body of water

a collection of poems and photos by
Chestina Craig

Copyright 2017 Chestina Craig
Book title credit to Alfredo Aguilar
Edited by Alfredo Aguilar, Sarah Thursday, and Sheila J Sadr
Cover model Dean Fryn
Cover photo by Chestina Craig
Layout and design by Sarah Thursday
ISBN-10: 0-9978155-5-8I
SBN-13: 978-0-9978155-5-9

table of contents

born swimming	1
on snorkeling in the cove where natalie wood drowned	2
family heirlooms	3
how to walk like a woman in the city	6
conversations with carbon	8
unnamed	10
north carolina 1998	11
question mark girl	12
windowless	14
catalina ii	15
him, burning	16
lead paintbrush	17
old poets	18
on men & also my ex	19
please don't leave me	20
cool girl	23
an ode to buffy the vampire slayer	25
us & the water	26
salt hum	28
I want to have the trust of a gray whale	29
girl	31
my baptism	32
previously published	34
thank yous	35

"How does the sea remember me. Every time."
—*Nayyirah Waheed*

born swimming

I love how we talk of evolution
like it is a choice,
say the shark got her teeth from
anything but necessity
from anything but her hunter's call—
that dilated pupil salt seer dance
I do not love how we speak of defense
like there is a choice between hook
in the gut & a snapped fishing line
when you steal the bait,
do not forget to smile.

on snorkeling in the cove where natalie wood drowned

we have made it here
on determination alone.
anchor down under the shadow of a drying
island / how many times
have we floated on top of death
& felt it?
how often, do we dedicate
our life to this—

is it natural for a giver like me
to love something that takes
so much?

they do not know
if / who
pushed her in,
I am here
with strangers.
I do not know
which of them would laugh
at me / the next drowning woman.

family heirlooms

For the women in my family
flame is an heirloom,
a tree made of kerosene—
we pass   a burning branch sewn to generations of consumption
parts of Salem,
holy-dug under our skin.
hundreds of years ago
the men propositioned my ancestor be burned
that she held her hands wide
in surrender
or in glory
& meet the fate
of a drying forest

I read of witches in my textbooks
touch the fate of them on the Fourth of July
fear the cacophony / the conflagration,
that towering body of tongues

the women in my family
burning witches
smart mouths
have always taught each other to reach across the tree canopy first,
let them know this
is how we dance

my great grandmother
used to cry about birds in her room:
red-breasted arson collapsing / the witches
in my family know things
before they happen
don't believe candles are power-tamed
but burnings lying in wait

the same as gas stoves,

how they showcased their affinity for bathrobes
& burning breakfasts on my grandmother—
my grandmother the bird,
a warm October bonfire taking   the left side of her body
the left side of my body is always
a little bit unwell
always hot to the touch
always trying to burn itself

the women in my family are incendiary
born lit match / born spell-caster
it is no coincidence we speak harsh,
walk like we aren't grounded
breathe holy & worship
how we keep warm.

how to walk like a woman in the city

Let your face say how
you carried a pocket knife as a girl / slipped & cut your leg
do not flinch,
walk too fast to be appetizing,
make your lover run after you
he is a man after all
& these are the things you are trying to avoid

one or ten matches slipped into
the side of your red socks—
enough friction in your smile
to burn his trespass,
not a body
just a snarling mouth
with things no one
wants to know about you.

conversations with carbon

I ask carbon, what does
it feel like to be backbone,
to have multiple arms,
to be mother
to all of me—Mother
to all of them

she says it is an honor
to hold all corners
of existence—an honor
to be skeleton

in everything

I ask her—
do you not feel stretched too thin
to never be all together
she says, what is structure if it cannot spread
why do we think together /
only means touching
she tells me

I know
what it is like to do thankless work
to be overlooked for gods

I ask her what is it like to feed fire,
she says he is a lost
child says he only ever wanted to become
asks if my skin, has heard him crying
into candles at night

tells me this is what it is
like to have your hand
pulled by the sun
she is the hand & the sun & the pulling

I ask her what is it like to be
ashes she says,

haven't
       you ever scattered
                       yourself

tells me to watch the leaves
on their way down
tells me loss isn't much different.

unnamed
[for Cole]

Do the stars in constellations miss each other / do they lament gravity / how he comes in like a god / collapsing creation / are they just glorified wounds / do they miss being unnamed / absent of eventual blood / want more of the astronomer's telescope / less of the moon think of her greedy / jealous how she transforms monthly / want to touch again / need more than us to just guess them / with finger lines / need more / than us.

north carolina 1998

I have these memories
my mother & I bleary eyed in your southern kitchen,
the cicadas chorus as you offer us toast
waking us jet-lagged
already dressed in your coffin,
that bathrobe.
I don't know if it was really there then but
I dress you in it every time you are alive
in my head it is not on fire
yet—

instead:
we are kneeling in the sand
(you-bathrobe
me-the bathing suit in all the pictures)
covered by each rolling wall of salt
water ragdoll up & down the beach laughing
it is my first memory of the ocean &
                                          we could just stay here
flame has no time for something so waterlogged

we could just
get a sunburn
instead.

question mark girl

When your first love
paints you into a box at sixteen
you will think sitting there,
is how to make men stay
forget how to ribbon joy from your throat
unless he tugs—
forget how to feel *anything*
but the gravity of another person.
when he yells at you to stop crying
tells you he loves you
& takes your hand to change the lightbulbs into
gaslights, you are already too in love*
*(too lost)

I am not a question mark girl
but he loved me that way
loved to watch me sit at the end of a sentence.
all spine   arched submissive.
deliberately packaged uncertain.
unable to ask / do you mean this

when he tells me
he slept with her,
mirrors my anger / back into my mouth,
I stay.
rip out my threads
to try to sew his broken
tell myself, this is different
this time
I will be better.
reckon myself angry boy doctor
feed this fever / starve in his cold
become a body thermometer,
talk him out of leaving every time
I see someone he, does not like.
become a starving garden,
can you photosynthesize anger
what crop do we make of this,

when he tells me, he hates my mother
I steal her cooking wine
stop singing in the car with her
& resent my best friend

when I finally leave him
I am more question mark girl than ever
curled skin on blank canvas,
knitting fingers dancing through dark—
spend years washing off all his red,
through new loves
where I clench my teeth
on how I feel, reach my hands out for too many boys
who could never love me
search for his anger in all of them & hope to find myself again
tucked down the voice in their throats
or spine
or bedsheets
but every time my open palms are still empty
of comfort after I have scraped it all clean.
I still hold malice & a joke in either hand
& cannot tell the difference—
shrink in the presence of both.

I am not his punctuation mark anymore
just a girl with an arched back
beginning to
unbend,

slowly taking up
stolen space.

windowless

There are too many poems
alive in this anatomy,
live wire begging
for a place to go—
name the fires talk
about the witch hunt but,

I do not own my hands or mouth today
could not call them by their right name
this body does not have enough person,
to spare.
 I shed skin
at each sunrise
& watch it name itself.

catalina ii

Some fish grind
their bones together to communicate,
I can understand missing
someone so much
that I would too.

him, burning

Compared to him, you were a sun
he is a lamp,
& when I look through my eyelids
it almost feels the same

                       except without any of the heat.

lead paintbrush

I am tired
of carrying this,
it's all consuming
ache the way it paints in reds & purples
how it bleeds so slowly never enough
to look quite the right color,
sometimes I feel it running
down my neck / can taste it
climbing up my throat / rosy as a thorn
they want me to shout but I never can convince my lungs
they deserve
the air / deserve the strain to get lost
to exhale the lead / the lost / the leaving
every time the forgetfulness has been a choice.
the ticking hands by the phone, the waiting
for the "I love you" call that never comes & when it does
I dress it differently, tell myself it's a liar.
look in the window / see the animal of my youth
tied to the chain link fence by her own sweater,
by her own friends,
better left rotting
than loved
better grind your own teeth together over forgiveness
better stay with the boy who lies like this is how he loves you
like this is how you belong
to him / better know he will make you
believe that this is all honest.
like the welts from this burning home
are paint / like the blood is paint,
you are the untrustworthy artist,
you are everything wrong with the way you have been treated
you are everything you feel about what has been done to you
which is undeserving / of a good love /
& not to feel
these vines around your arms that taste like salt & goodbye
& save me / to everyone around you
as they watch you
feast upon them.

old poets

I want to be like them
more than my professors.
to have Sunday night
translate into possibilities,
they tell me my name sounds like how a persimmon looks,
they say who wants to go scream at god in a bar.
I have only been old enough for two months
I already know I am either screaming—
Thank
 you
 —or—
Fuck you
I don't know which is worse.

on men & also my ex

1. A comedian makes a joke
about buying dinner & not
getting her mouth
in return,
the punch line is
a body belonging to itself.

2. You don't know how much you miss him,
until you think a stranger is his smile
& in this you realize
you are always mistaking telephone poles
for crosses.

3. I once dated a boy
who loved my deep conditioner.
I would overuse it,
saturate my hair in coconut silently,
thankless.
I wonder why I am always softening
myself
for men.

4. I don't remember why
I spent a year of my life on a boy
who only told me I was beautiful,
with his hands.

please don't leave me

I carve a three-story mansion out of my bones
whether he asks for it or not / this time
I am lucky
that he makes the bed & wants to know
what he can do to keep the place
together / takes me home
across his hands, invites me
to sit

not long after the paint dries
I start apologizing for the loose
floorboards, which is to say,
what makes me feel walked upon—
    which is to say my baggage.
speak more "I'm sorry" than
"thank you's", fear every frown
is how he begins to leave me,
remember how the screen door sounded

last time
someone left, let it play on repeat in my hallways.
tangle with what it means
to lock
& unlock my own body at night,
wonder why the only metaphor I can make
of this fear always
builds me as a house.
like I am vacant
fixer upper, somewhere to be lived in,
meaningless without
    people / share all my loving
with fear.

like I step too heavy in their bodies
leave too many
scuff marks & threaten
combustion, second guessing
the home I market—the whole of me,

the weight of clinging to everything,
afraid to be empty of breathing
besides the wind whistling through.

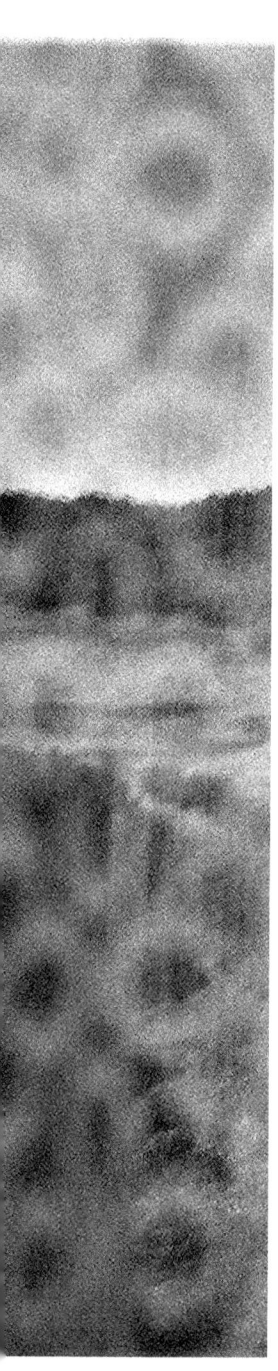

cool girl
[after Gillian Flynn's Gone Girl]

Boys want a Cool
Girl they can clean their teeth with.
fresh pick that tired smile
ask you,
        to unbirth the water
tell a joke with only sharp edges to suck
the surge inside your cavities.
web net the sounds, the bile
that sewages a hole in your bedsheets

Cool Girl swallows
every word that doesn't taste like sugar.
what is a Cool Girl, if she does not go down
smoothly / does not glint
marble any other style
but softly,
like she's got an oiled jaw
that presses into bear trap smiles
during poker games where boy's
boyish-friends make laughter about her body
lifeless, at the bottom of the backyard cliff
& the boy smiles & the Cool Girl stares ahead
 & bites
her blood.

an ode to buffy the vampire slayer

& here you are archetypal blonde
short skirt / cherry candy / the-first
to-die-kind-of-girl
the-first-to-be-punished for those
extra inches of sunlight, coming
into your body
you already did.
those heels / stake tongue,
the way your hair bounces
after you swing your fist.
how delicate your hands look
around the throat,
of a thing that thought it could
take you,
thought you could be its first bloodlet,
a personal drought
you are no riverbed
they don't know what lip gloss can do for this cracked earth.

& here you are twisted ankle
blue eye shadow name joke on every letterman's lips.
but you are still there every time they scream.
you are still Athena on the hunt,
chariot in like a demon's gravestone—
what does it mean to be evil's bad dream
& here you are praying for its retraction
how do you carry your love out
of the fire line dressed up on you.
does it weigh like this planet
your job would have you die on,
how you dance with fate & here you are

bloody & moon phase bruised,
always something smoky, warped
like hot metal.
always crisis just sheered on your teeth,
always shoulders out, crossbow shaped
you knee high boots / cheer leader try out
apocalypse-kind-of-girl.

us & the water
[for Brooke]

I half grew up in my childhood friend's home
we shared every body of water
like a secret: (the hot tub)
(our swimming lessons)—
which is to say, how we learned to survive
(lifeguarding)—which is to say how we learned
to save each other
(the ocean)—something we are so good at flinging
our bodies into,
this the salt womb we share,
the song we return to every warm
season, smelling of sunscreen
& sisters, this multitude:
I am crashing at the surface
& she is all the deep,
every undertow, every lung full of brine.
we always scatter head first
into the sand or billowing riptide,
always pull the other's hand as hard as the current—
march against it like a game.
us & the water
know every age we've ever been.

salt hum

In the mirror is a girl
made of too many
overswallowed metaphors
part of the ocean that stole itself away
    from home, only knows
grace where she cannot breathe
hunts those with only broken glass to give   eats
  it all until she coughs up salt,
coughs up smoothed tiny pieces of darkness,
coughs up a beating heart /   her hands,
try to share them like rolling tides
—is a rolling tide dressed human
wants to be the sun / a star / explosions
instead drops the moon out of gaping lips.
cannot burn skin,
    can be stared at for too long.
silver like a spoon for eating,
like server only meaningful
              to mouths.

I want to have the trust of a gray whale
[for Lauren]

Before whales were protected
hunters descended upon a lagoon in Baja
held strong by new mothers &
did not let them become
old mothers.

today in this lagoon,
whales approach
fishing boats they could easily bury
beneath them & instead lift their young
above the water for human hands to touch.

I want to have the trust of a gray whale,
to hold my entire core
out to something that looks so much like what defeated me last
& trust
nothing can hurt me
this time.

girl
[after Trista Mateer]

I used to think girl meant pink
meant birthday cake flowers,
be pretty for safety & always
use your inside voice, but sometimes
it means shout and they will still ignore you
means car key fingers, take me seriously,
never flinch, bitchface.
means don't fucking touch me
knife-in-boot confidence
painted fingernails and using them means
their dirt, being your own garden
means this
isn't always mine.

sometimes the bravest thing
is to walk down an alley alone,
sometimes girl
is synonymous with prey, means hunted,
means unafraid
of the dark, afraid of what's in it. girl
means getting used to this.
means kiddie pool and peach juice,
innocence as currency, fake flower sleepovers
strong hand on the back of your neck at the theater
girl just wanted to watch the movie
sometimes girl means cry,
means swelling mascara, lipstick
in the darkest shade you can buy,
no shame in smearing.
means shame. means always fighting the instinct
to shrink.

sometimes girl means shrinking,
sometimes means fighting
girl always means magic, always means
blessing, girl always makes
magic. means this space belongs
right here. girl belongs in magic.
means belong. girl
belongs.

my baptism

I pick what I want it to be every time
each new God a mouth on my ear
always burning / only listening for what I want
sometimes
it is calloused hands / taking me / to where
they have played a song & felt
like this could be home / do not stop
to speak all the best
gifts are silent skin

touching / sometimes it is underwater / when my lungs
feel like they might balloon out of my body &
leave me in the rocks, laughing, pressurized
kissing abalone into my nerve endings &

sometimes I stomp my feet
so hard
the little bones break / the little bones don't have names but
love a sacrifice for feelings / for a dance
when I am so expanded it can only come out
when everything else around me is loud & crying &
asking you also to move
your hands like his hands
& the salted ocean your heart
is so buoyant in / a life raft

you are always seeped into something
you want to be / holy, cleansed over & over
by something new
some other girl, some other home, a new deity
a new prayer / you are no statue I can worship
whatever makes me pry
myself
open

previously published

Thank you to the editors of the following publications where versions of these poems first appeared:

"how to walk like a woman in the city" —September 2016 in *The Rising Phoenix Review*

"conversations with carbon" —June 2016 in *The Metaworker*

"question mark girl" —July 2017, a previous version in video format, by *Button Poetry*

"old poets" & a previous version of "on men and also my ex" —September / October 2016 in *L'Ephemere Review*

"cool girl" - published in Rising Phoenix review, August 2017

"us & the water" —May / June 2017 in *L'Ephemere Review*

"girl" —July 2016 in *The Metaworker* & *Kings Zine* (Issue 1)

thank yous

First and foremost, thank you, Sarah Thursday and Sadie Girl Press for willingly giving a home to my words. I value your dedication to this & the community.

My family, thank you for being scientific & artistic. I love this duality. I love that I have it too.

Brooke, for loving the ocean as much as I do. Here's to 20 more years of friendship.

Santa Cruz Word Church, Definitive Soapbox, Uncultivated Rabbits, & Glassless Minds, thank you for being places that I do not sleep but are home all the same.

Thank you, Alfredo, for the thoughtful title & edits. I am proud to be your friend.

Cole & Sam, for getting it. I adore you both tremendously. I would make music with you any day.

Thank you, Jay, my partner, for reminding me that I am okay when I don't feel like I am.

Sheila, Stephanie, and Lauren, you will be my teammates forever.

My wonderful biology ladies, Megan, Alison, Alex, Rhea, Zoe, & Leigh, thank you for not judging me for writing awkward poems during study sessions and supporting my endeavors even though poetry has no p-values.

Brandon and Farah, for being two of the people who emulate the most warmth & for saying nice things about me.

Thank you, Antonio, for being a better mentor than I could ever ask for.

Edwin, you are the best coach. I look up to you so much.

Dean, for letting me photograph you.

Thank you, Wilton, you're the best cat.

& the ocean, for everything.

about the author

Chestina Craig lives in Long Beach, CA with her cat. Her work has been published in Black Napkin Press, The Rising Phoenix Review, KINGS ZINE, L'EPHEMERE Review, Femme Fotale (photography), Button Poetry, and others. She has presented her work at The President's Commission on The Status of Women, The Young Women's Empowerment Conference, The CSUF Social Justice Summit, Glassless Minds Open Mic, The Santa Cruz Word Church, and more. She also has a bachelor's degree in Marine Biology, and on occasion pets sharks and hangs out with octopuses. Other talents include winning over the love of cats, eating whole pizzas, and falling in love with the glow of the sunset. She hopes that one day she will only be required to wear gauzy clothing, swim in the ocean's swell, and get paid to have too many feelings. Find out more on chestinacraig.com.

www.ingramcontent.com/pod-product-compliance
Lightning Source LLC
Chambersburg PA
CBHW070043070426
42449CB00012BA/3152